merlot merlittle

The joy of wine

Published by Last Lemon Productions
60 Woodside Dr. San Anselmo,
CA 94960, USA

ISBN 978-1-7332675-1-9

First Printing, 2019

www.lastlemon.com

This book
is for

Hello,

Have you met Harold? He's our bobbly-nosed, soft-footed hero, beloved to many through the Harold's Planet greeting cards (millions of which have been sold around the world since 1999) and the stream of new cartoons seen on thousands of screens every day.

But there's nothing quite like a book, is there? And there's no theme dearer to Harold's heart, than the simple joy of wine.

So - cheers, salud, skål, Å'kålè ma'luna, cin cin, lechyd da, na zdorovie, fe sahetek, santé, prost, l'chaim, sláinte and gesondheid in die rondheid - enjoy!

Lisa + Ralph

Lisa Swerling + Ralph Lazar

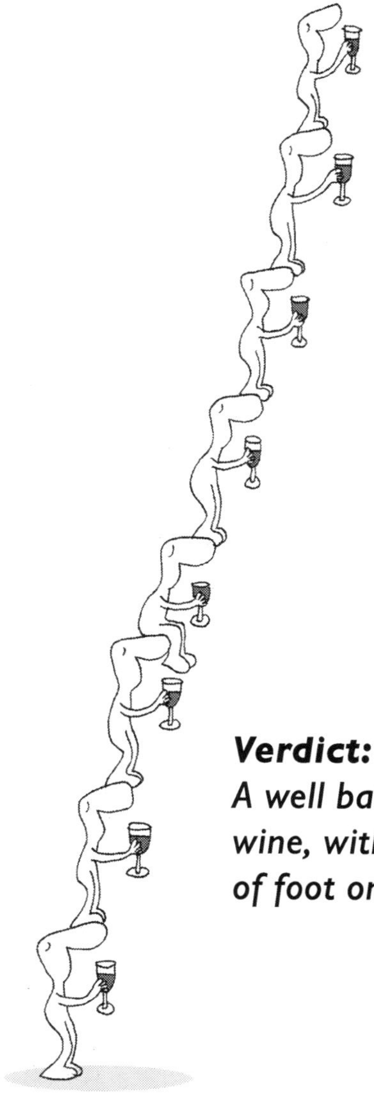

Verdict:

A well balanced wine, with a hint of foot on the nose.

HOW TO *STAY MOTIVATED*

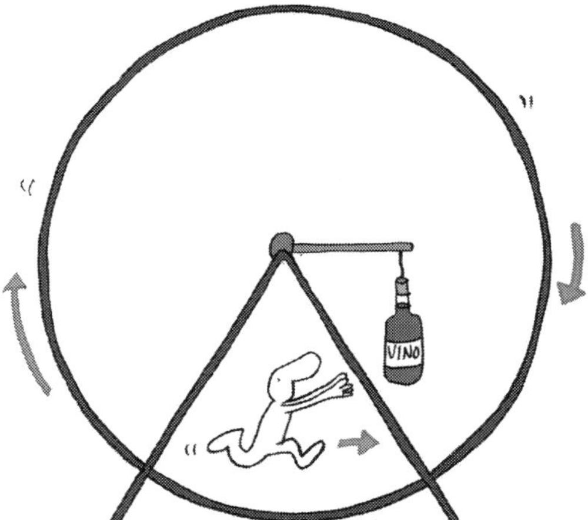

Sauvignon
Blanc
Shiraz
Rosé
Pinot
Gris

Cycling for wine-lovers

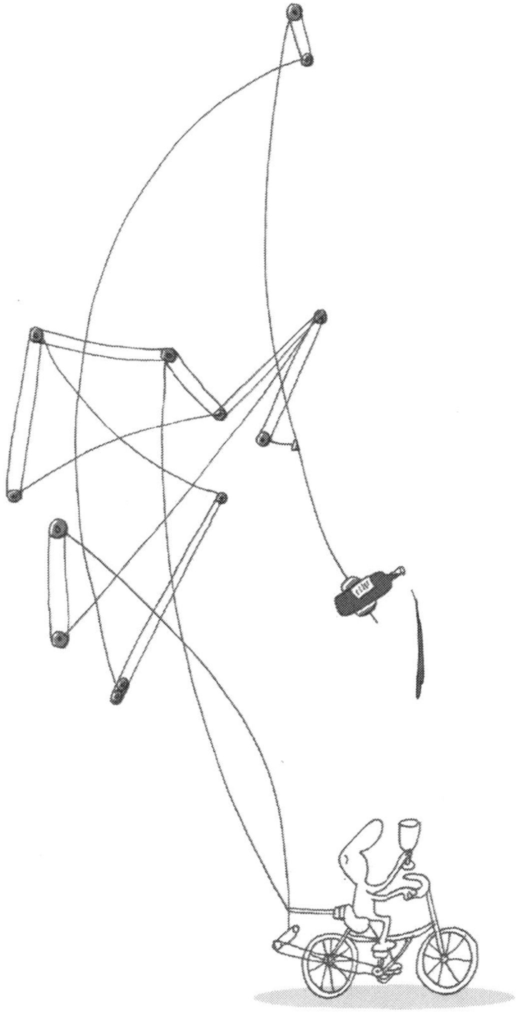

COFFEE KEEPS ME SANE

UNTIL IT'S ACCEPTABLE

TO DRINK WINE

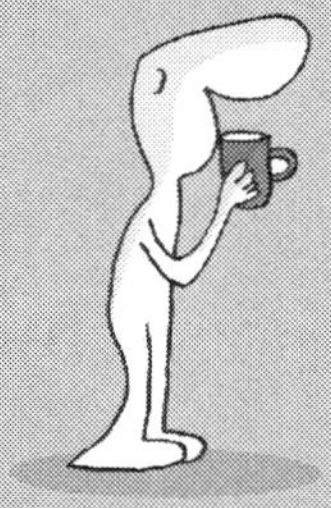

La vie
en rosé

BORDEAUX

The MERLOTBULANCE

PILATES
FOR PEOPLE WHO LOVE WINE

The Lost Winery
of Atlantis

That's what friends are for...

Life is a little odd.

You're a little odd.
I'm a little odd.

That's why we get on so well...

A tantalising leak in the wine storage facility

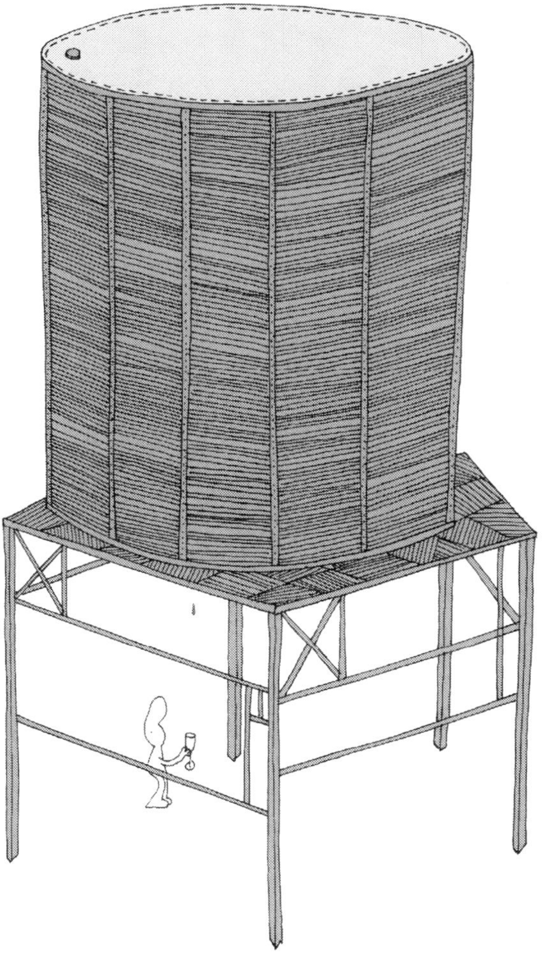

Latin Basics: *Lesson I*

HAPPINESS IS...

YOU + ME +
A COUPLE OF
GLASSES OF WINE

Don't forget to let it breathe

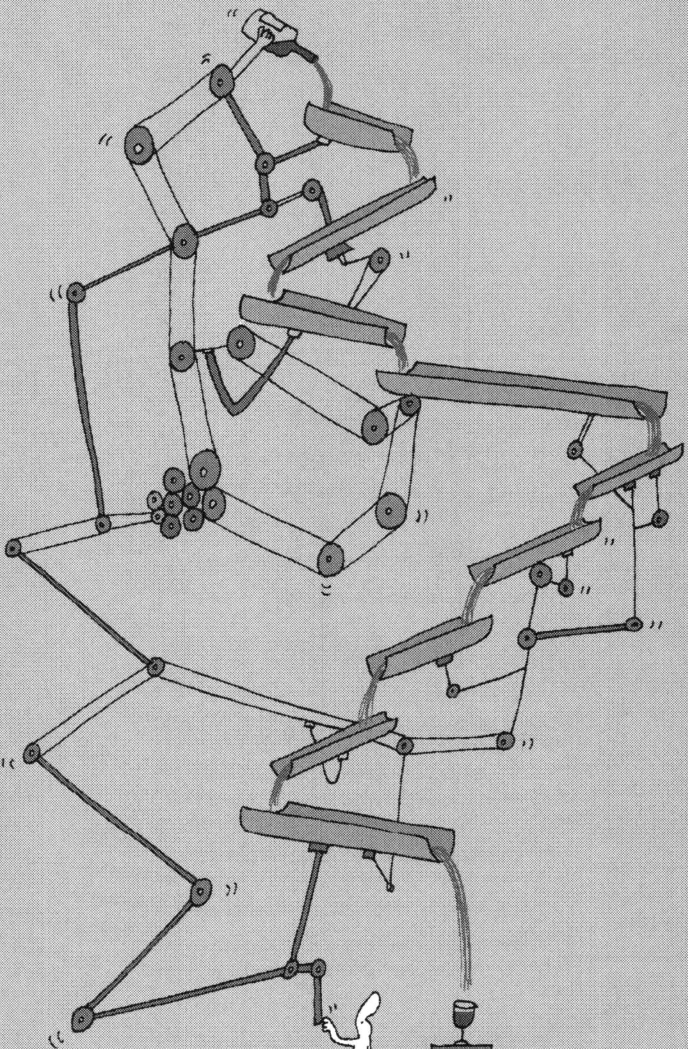

The traveling Pinot salesmen

Yoga for Winelovers

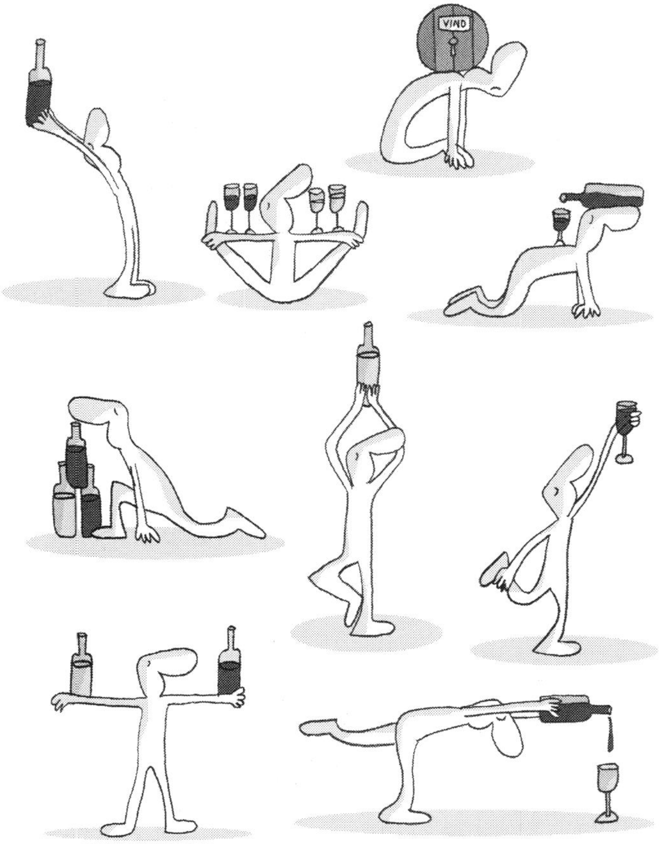

ALSO AN ANIMATION! www.lastlemon.com/harolds-planet/animations

The Great Outdoors

How to *Appreciate Wine*

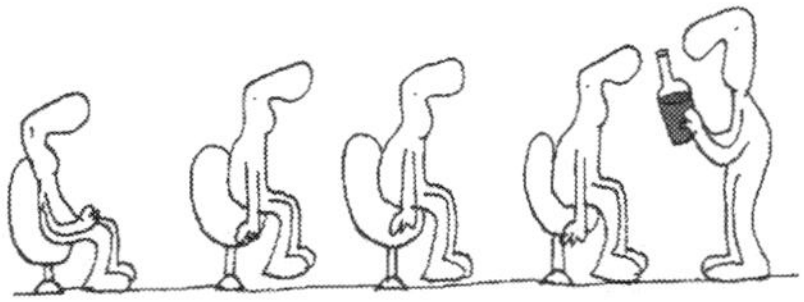

(1) *Attend a history of wine lecture.*

(2) *Attend a wine-tasting course.*

(3) *Watch documentaries on the subject.*

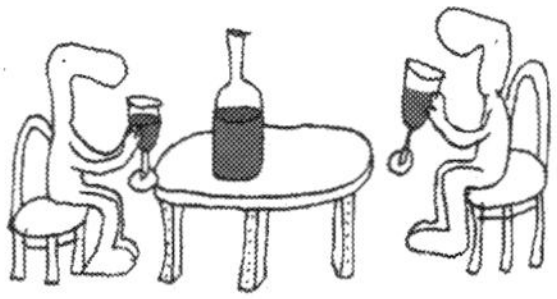

(4) *Buy a bottle and drink it with someone nice.*

A robust red wine
is IRREFUTABLE PROOF
that someone upstairs
wants us to be happy...

KINDS OF LOVE

Love of
fellow humans

Love of
coffee

Love of
latte

Love of
espresso

Love of
hairiness

Love of
wine

Love of
buttocks

Love of
garlic

Love of
carrot juice

def. **LAGOM**:

Swedish (adj.): Just the right amount.

ODE TO CHEESE AND WINE

LET THERE BE
CHEESE
& WINE

And if that's too much to ask
Don't bother with the cheese

Breakthroughs in Technology:

The ability to download wine off the Internet

You Can Do Anything

as long as you have a compass, a pen-knife, some string, cheese, **wine**, *several credit cards, a few million dollars in your bank account, a private helicopter, and tissues...*

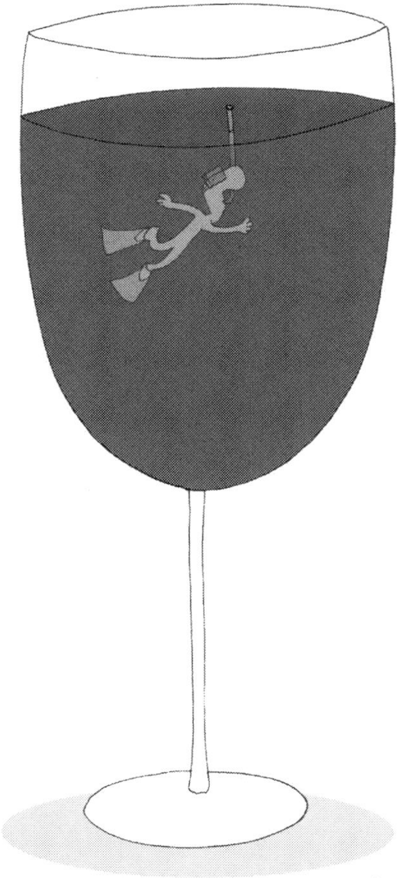

Some days are just

Standing-Quietly-With-a Decent-Syrah-On-Head-Days*

**If bottle gets heavy, by all means make it easier for yourself by partaking of some, or sharing it with someone nice.*

Rumors of red
wine rain...

Harold's Handy Gadget #13

LAST ORDERS FACILITATOR

(makes sure you never miss last orders)

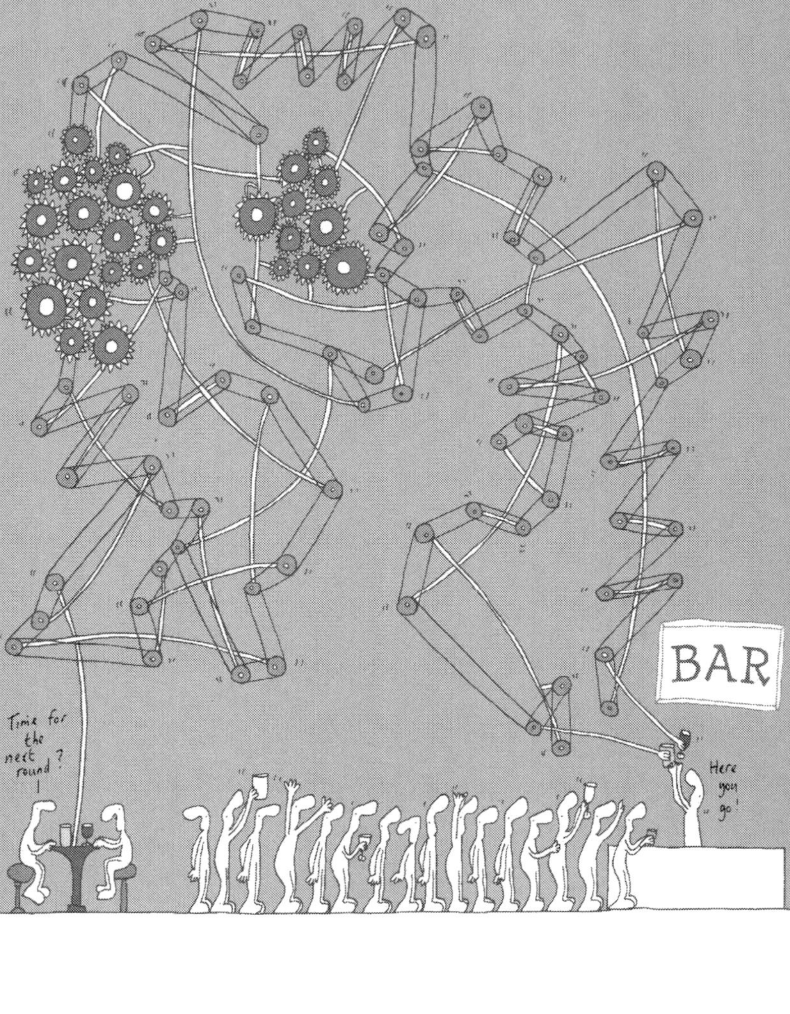

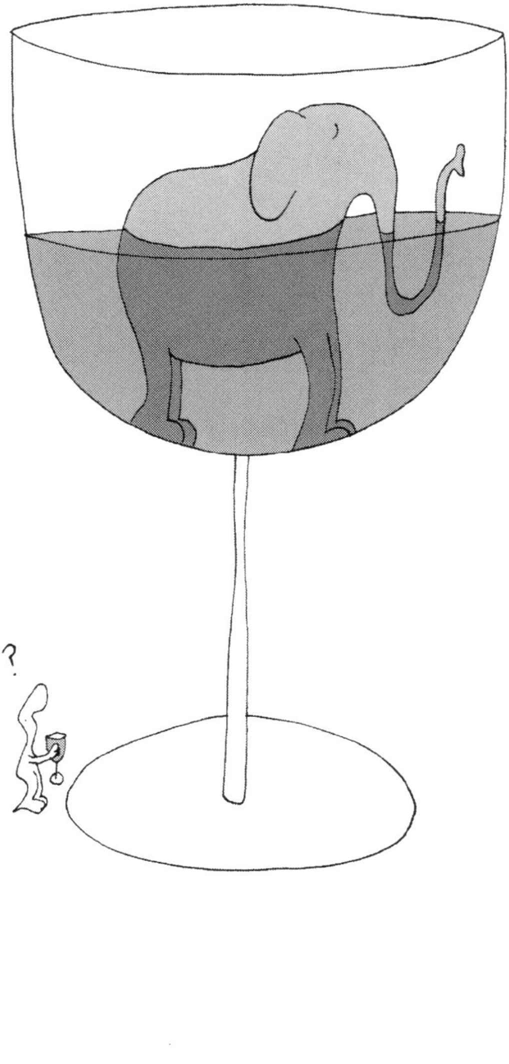

Why do I always carry a corkscrew with me?

Well, it's in case a lovely little bottle of Zinfandel comes trotting past....

How to *Make your Tap-water Taste Better*

1 *Fill glass with water.*

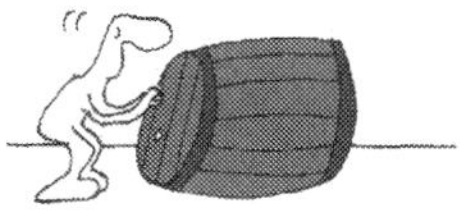

2 *Get large barrel of Cabernet Sauvignon.*

3 *Pour glass of water into barrel.*

4 *Decant equivalent of one glass.*

5 *Tastes much better, doesn't it?*

DIVE BAR
COCKTAIL LOUNGE
ALE HOUSE
SALOON
WINE BAR
PUB
?

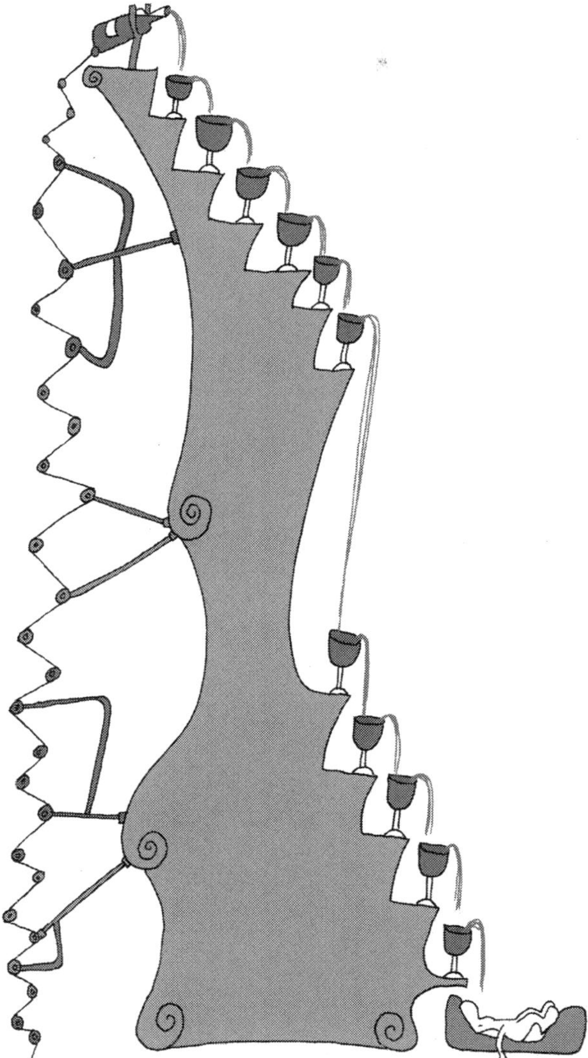

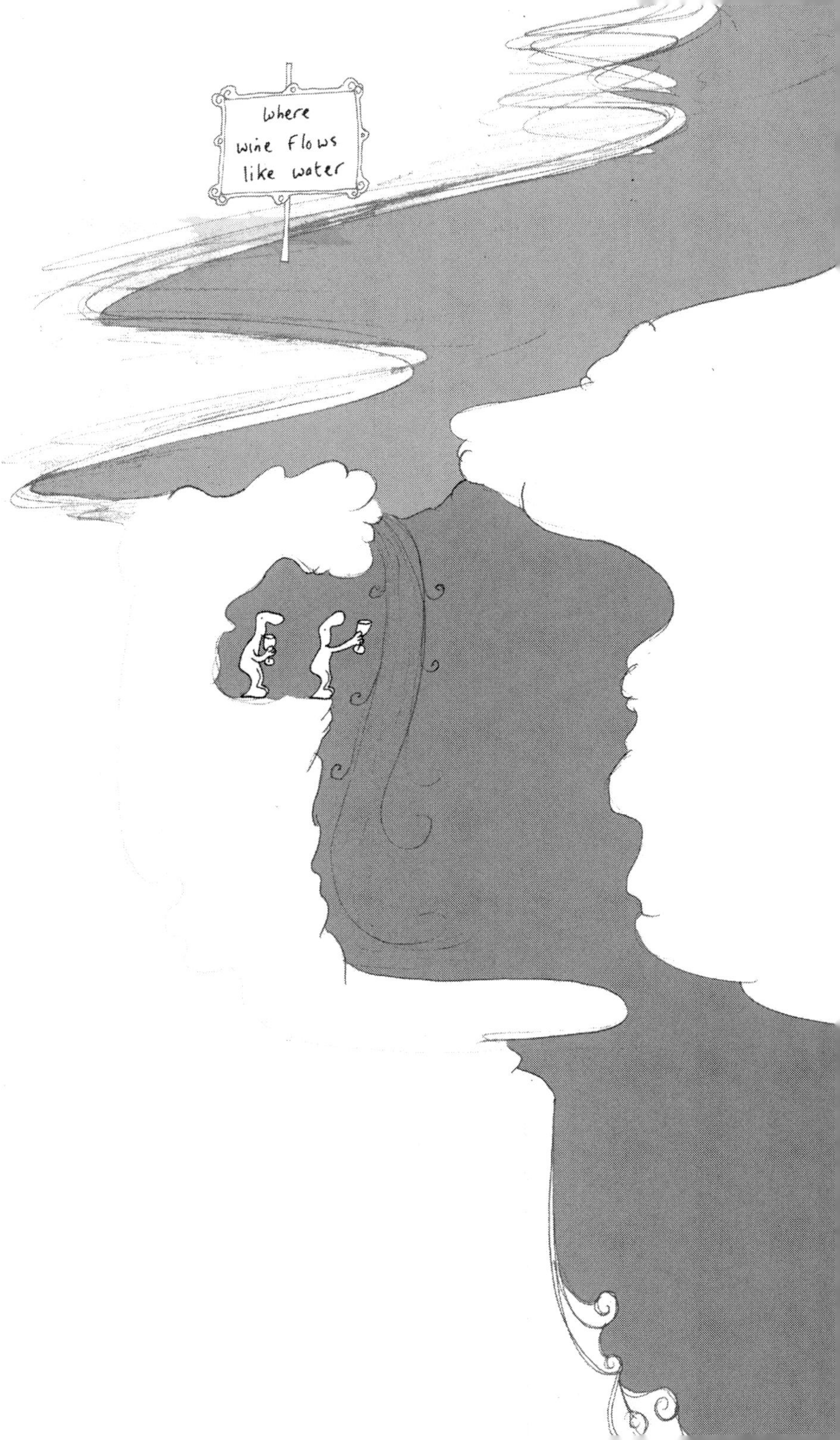
where
wine flows
like water

NOTHING BETTER THAN A GOOD FRIEND*

**except a good friend who has wine*

Regular day

Red Wine Day

Red Nose Day

Red Wine
Red Nose Day

Def. **NOVINOPHOBIA**
The fear of running out of wine.

Bicycle Varietals
for White Wine Lovers

Sauvignonblancycle

Chardonnaycycle

Rieslingcycle

Laws of Nature #17

There's no such thing as too much red wine

Proseccacophony

How to *Appreciate Wine*

Open bottle.

Pour into glass.

Sip.

Say appreciative things.

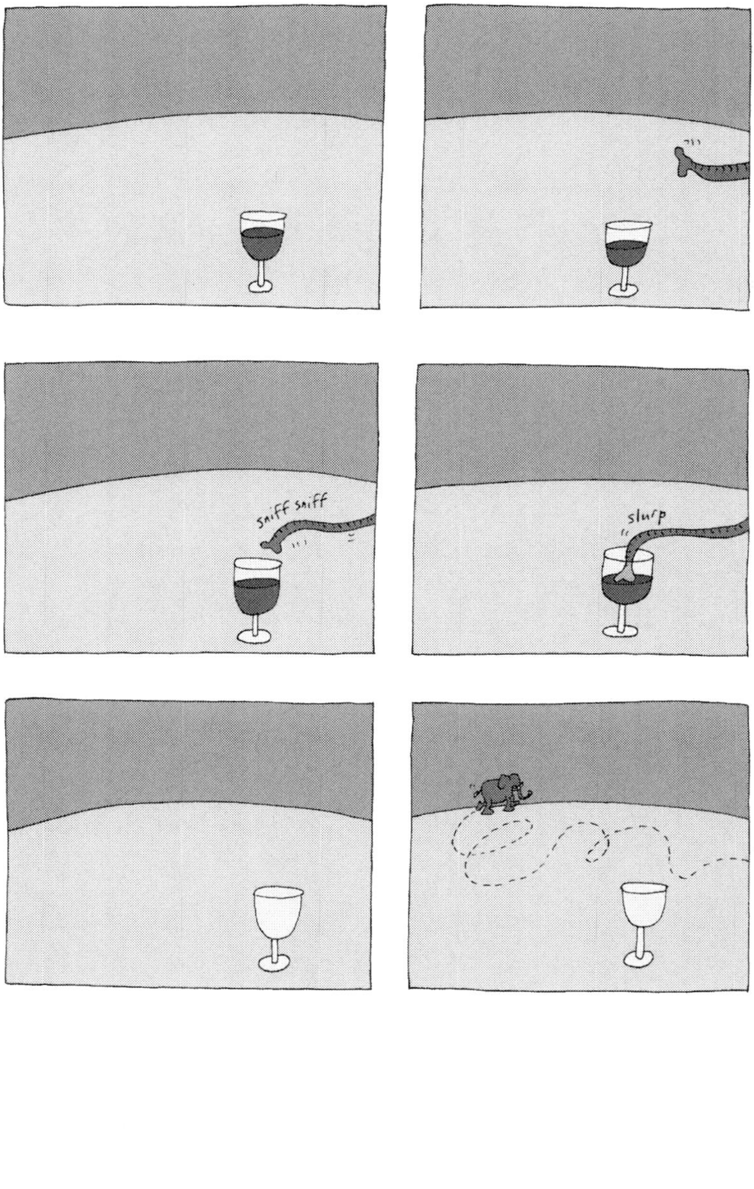
sniff sniff
slurp

Stay inspired

IN CASE OF EMERGENCY

BREAK GLASS

Small house,
BIG cellar

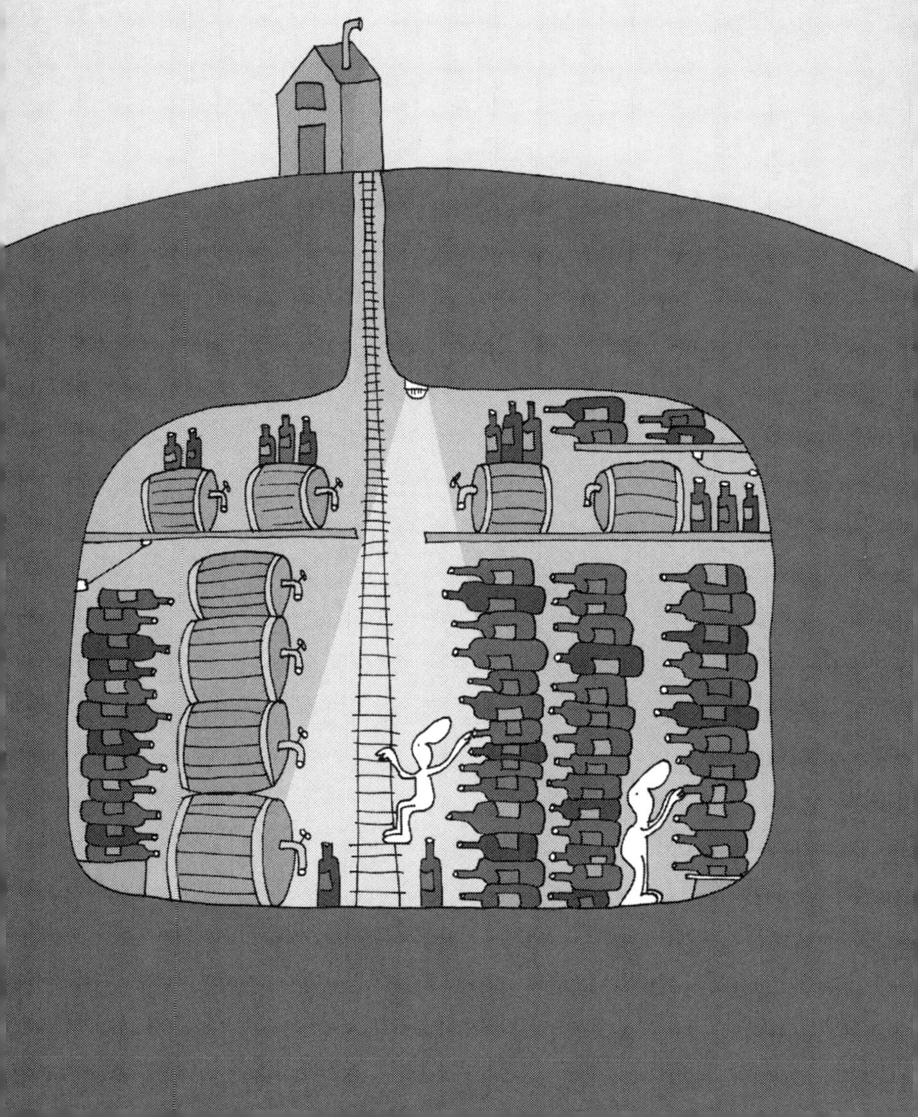

There's nothing quite like getting together over a bottle of wine and chatting about nothing in particular...

Group Therapy

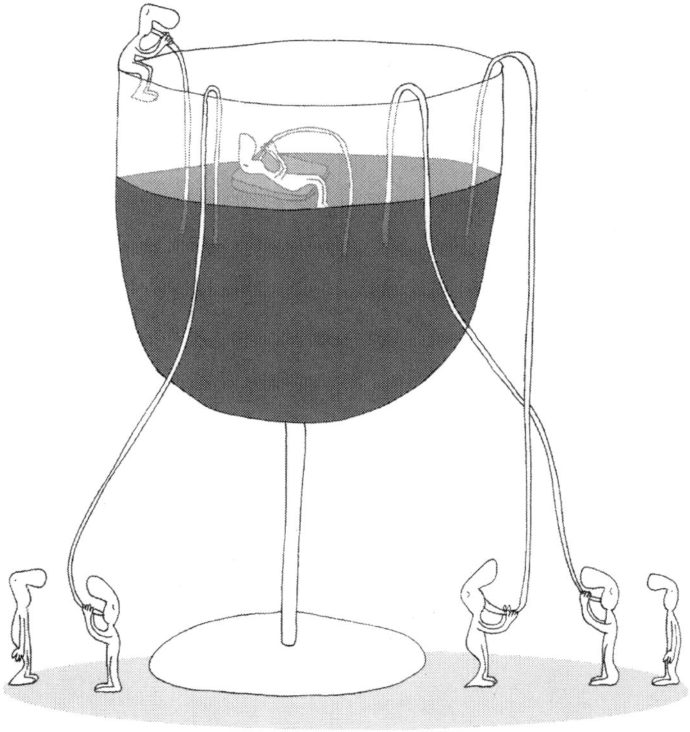

Glass
Half Full or
Half Empty?

Who knows?
Who cares?

Harold's Handy Gadget #14

THE TELEPATHIC DRINK SERVER

(serves you the perfect drink, at just the right moment)

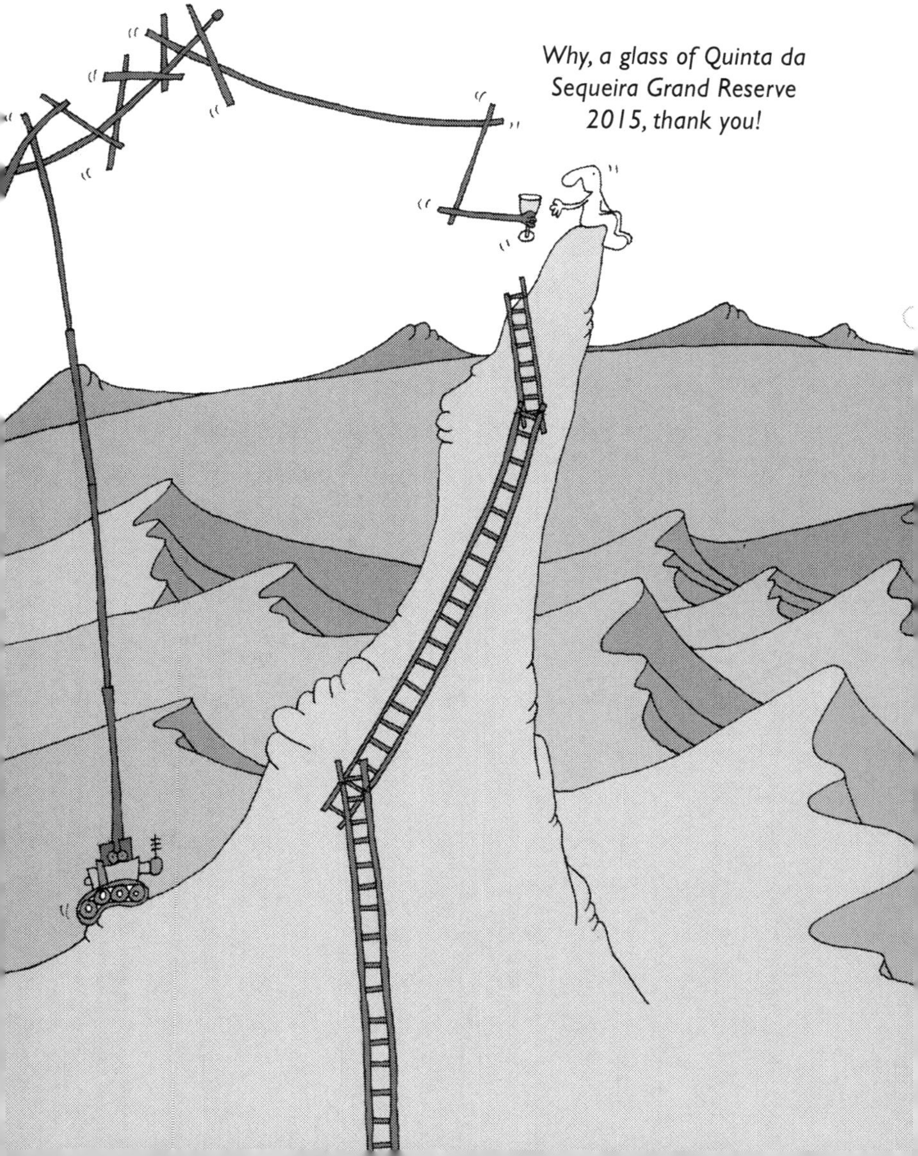

The privilege of friendship is to talk total nonsense, and have that nonsense respected

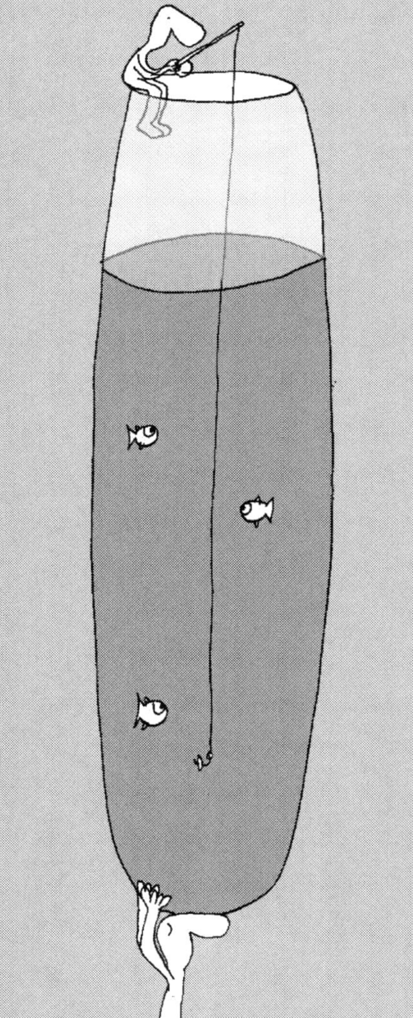

An Exceptionally
Merry Christmas

YOU ONLY LIVE ONCE...

...but if you do it with
good cheese & decent wine,
once is enough...

ROLL ON
THE GOOD
TIMES!

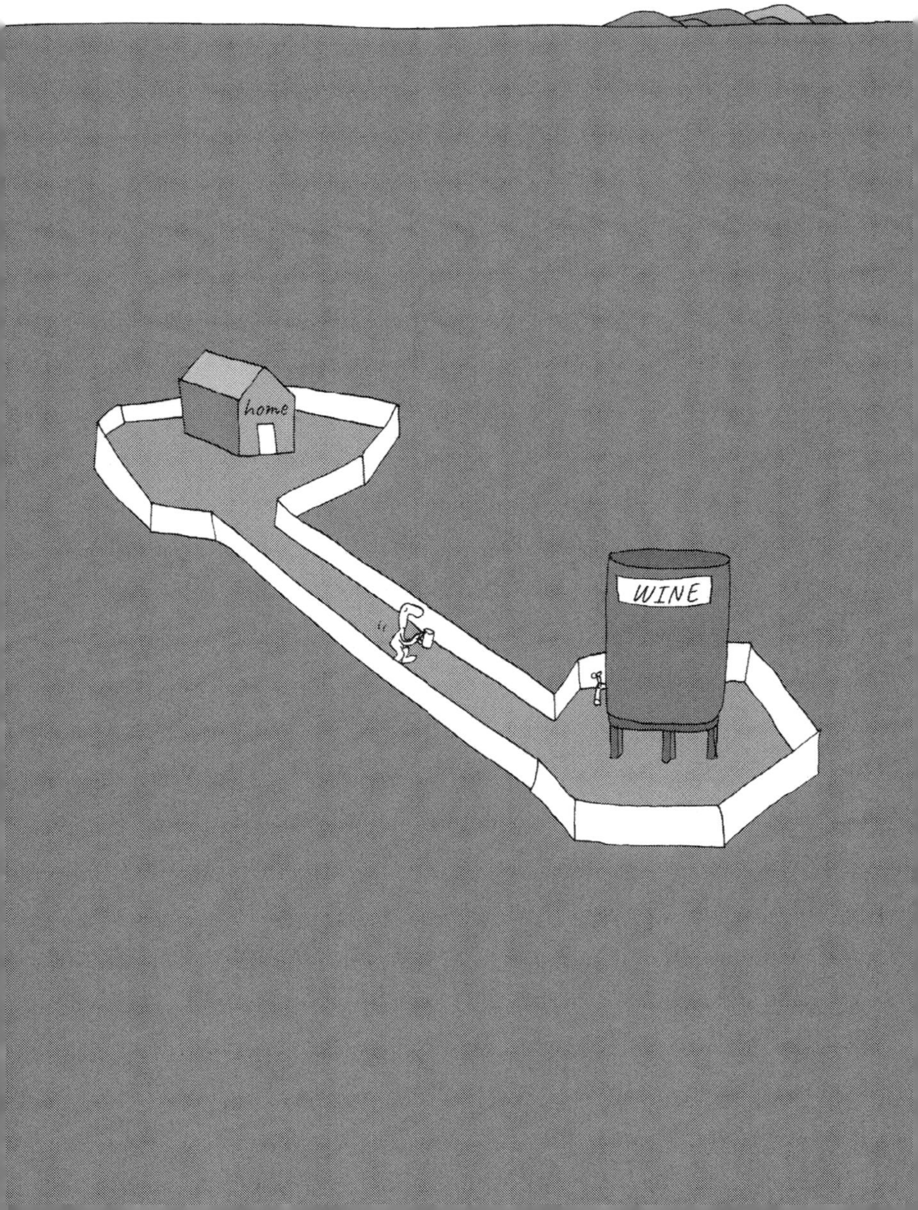
home
WINE

FRIENDSHIP, WINE AND LAUGHTER

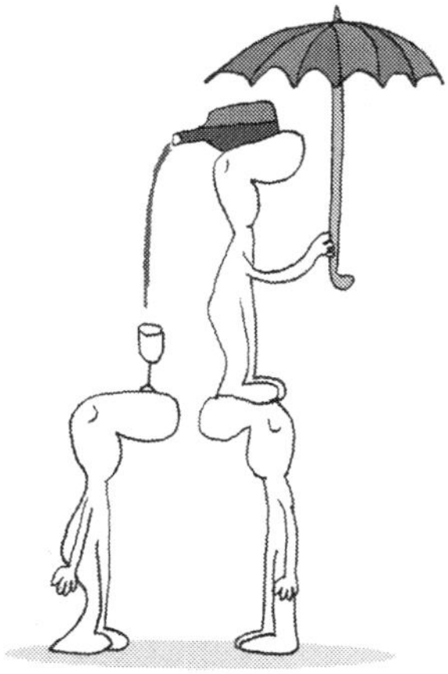

Who could ask for more?

Hat Trick

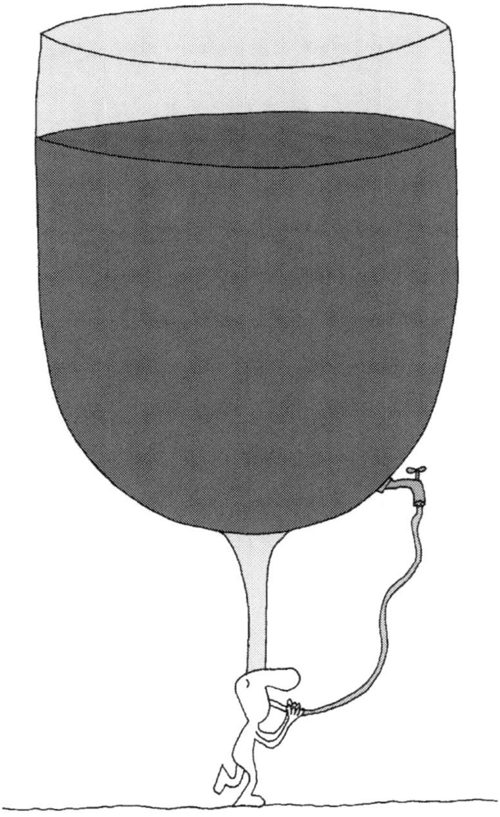

On the Open Plain that is Life,
what could be more welcome
than a little something to drink?

PORT

Decisions, decisions

How to *Save Water:* *Drink Wine*

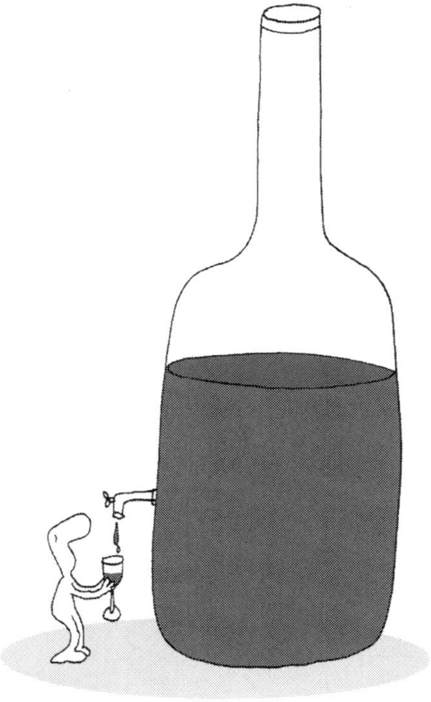

The wine delivery van is late and everyone is starting to get a bit twitchy

Feet up and wine down

Always the show-off

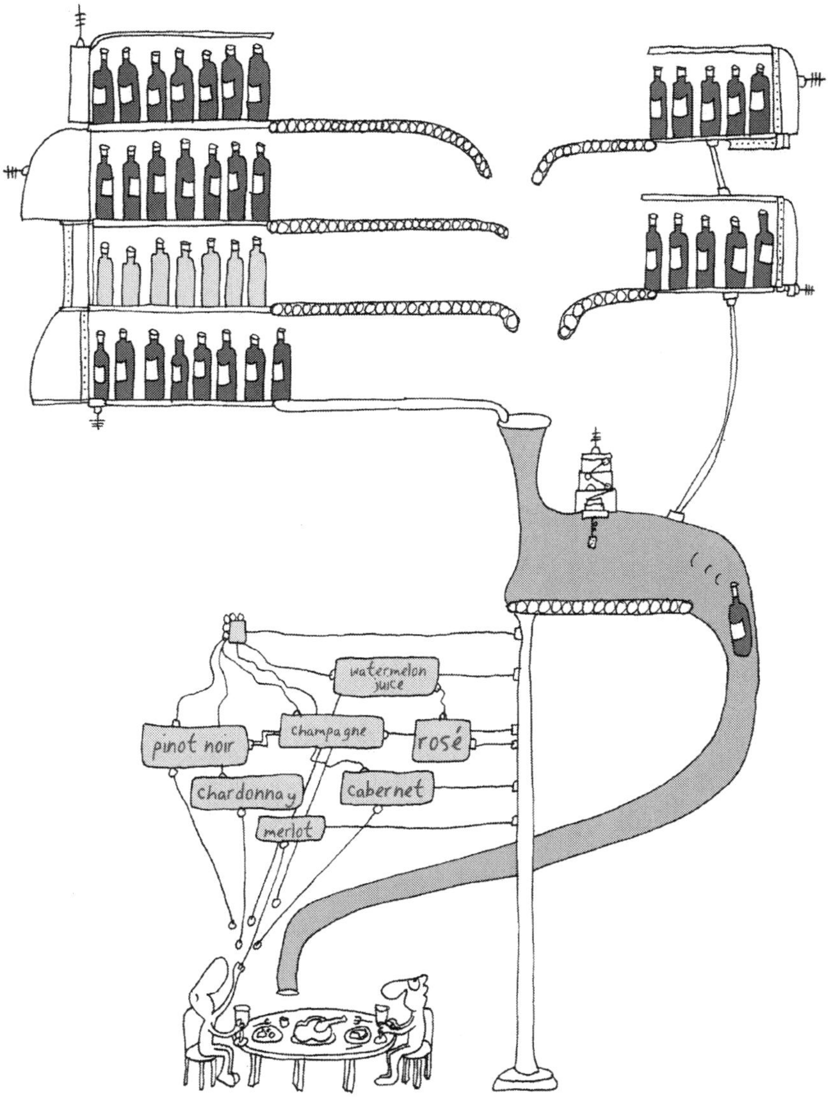

Uses of Rhinoceroses #1
Wine Storage

Books & time, that's all I need...

Never give up

The perfect storm

BORDEAUX

"It is one of the blessings of old friends that you can afford to be stupid with them."

-Ralph Waldo Emerson

*May you grow old and wise like a noble oak, and may you mature to perfection like a fine red wine**

**An effective way to ensure this outcome is to go have a glass of wine in a tree right now...*

Signs of Life on Mars

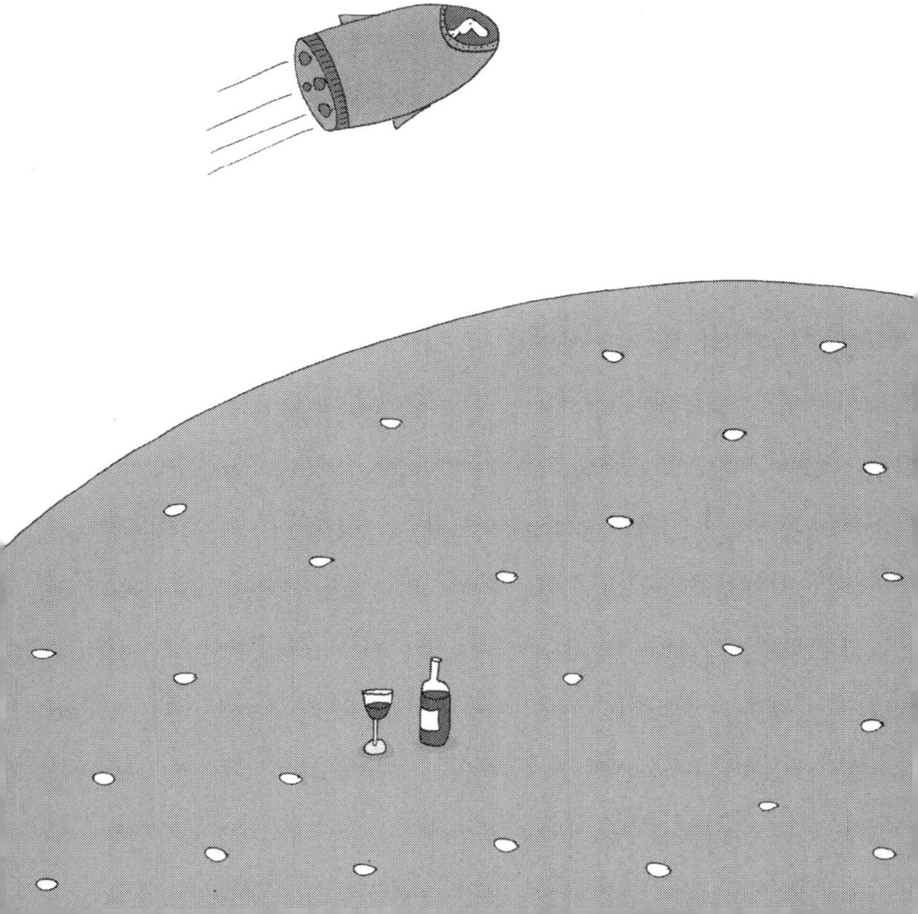

And finally....let's sail away on a sea of Beaujolais...

ABOUT THE AUTHORS

Lisa Swerling & Ralph Lazar live in California.

They are the creators of the popular illustrated project ***Happiness Is...****, which has sold nearly half a million books and has over three million followers online.*

They also wrote and illustrated the New York Times bestseller ***Me Without You*** *and two other* **HAROLD'S PLANET** *books* ***Smile*** *and* ***Be Afraid,*** *available on Amazon.*

VISIT HAROLD ONLINE

There is a huge library of Harold's Planet cartoons online at
www.lastlemon.com/harolds-planet

facebook.com/itsharoldsplanet
instagram.com/harolds.planet

29146372R00054

Printed in Great Britain
by Amazon